A TRIP TO JEREMYVILLE
coloring book

A TRIP TO JEREMYVILLE
coloring book

Andrews McMeel Publishing®
a division of Andrews McMeel Universal

A Trip to Jeremyville Coloring Book
copyright © 2016 by Jeremyville. All rights reserved.
Printed in China. No part of this book may be used or
reproduced in any manner whatsoever without written permission
except in the case of reprints in the context of reviews.

Andrews McMeel Publishing
a division of Andrews McMeel Universal
1130 Walnut Street, Kansas City, Missouri 64106

www.andrewsmcmeel.com

16 17 18 19 20 SHZ 10 9 8 7 6 5 4 3 2 1

ISBN: 978-1-4494-7774-5

ATTENTION: SCHOOLS AND BUSINESSES
Andrews McMeel books are available at quantity discounts with
bulk purchase for educational, business, or sales promotional use.
For information, please e-mail the Andrews McMeel Publishing
Special Sales Department: specialsales@amuniversal.com.

BECOME A CHAMPION OF YOUR OWN GAME.

GROW LOVE DAILY.

FIND YOUR CLEARING IN THE FOREST.

OUR ETERNITY IS WITHIN.

CELEBRATE ALL THE LAYERS WITHIN YOU.

WE'LL MEET SOME DAY IN THE SO FAR AWAY.

CHOOSE HAPPINESS INSTEAD.

BREAK OUT THE VEGETABLE MOVES.

NATURE IS THE GREATEST STORY EVER WRITTEN.

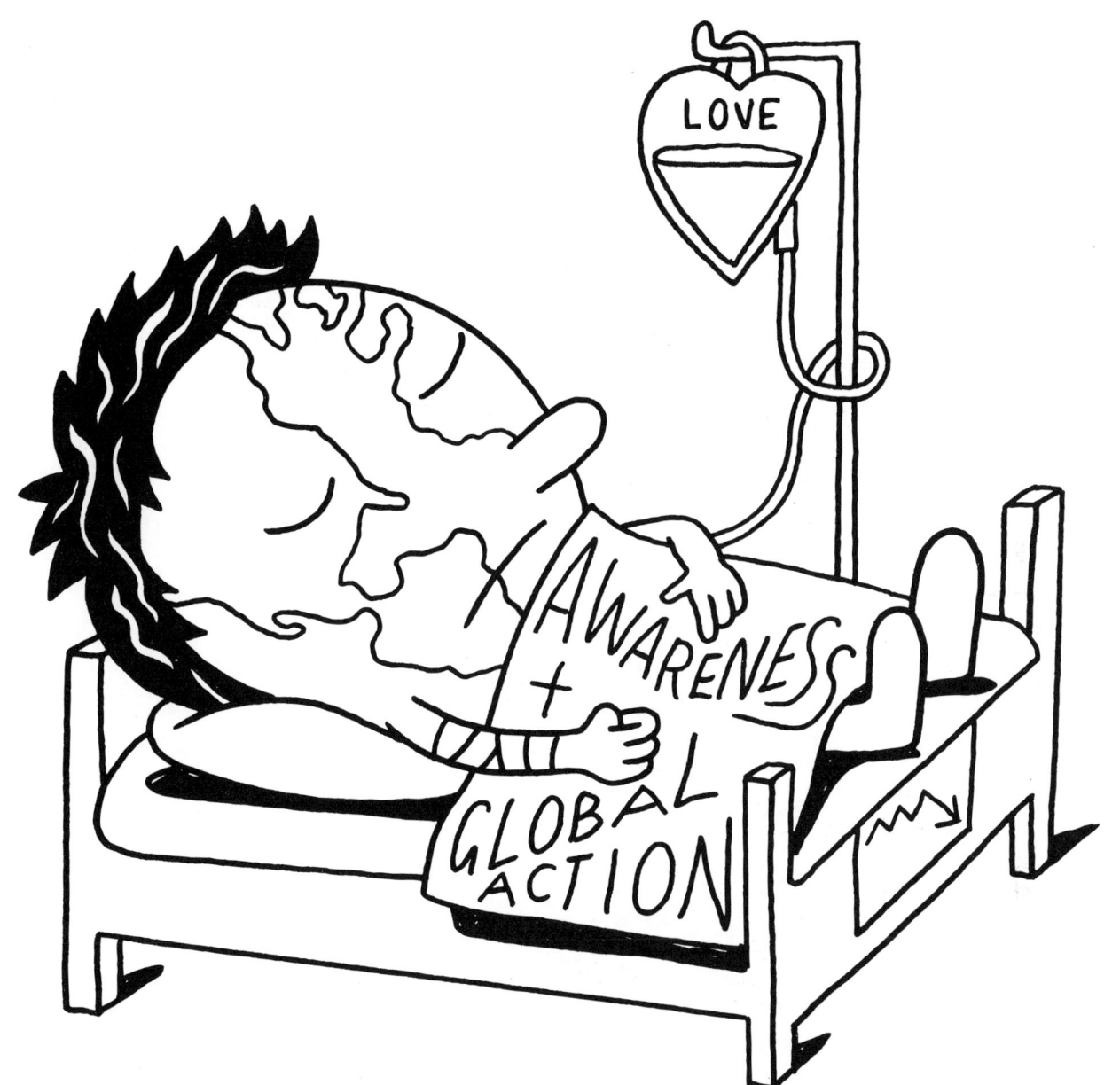

BELIEVE IN YOU.

CREATE THE STARS IN YOUR NIGHT.

CHANGE YOUR CIRCUMSTANCE.